Explore
Music
through
Maths

David Wheway and
Shelagh Thomson

22 varied national curriculum
Music activities linked to the
Maths attainment targets

Music Department
OXFORD UNIVERSITY PRESS
Oxford and New York

Oxford University Press, Walton Street, Oxford OX2 6DP, England

Oxford is a trade mark of Oxford University Press

First published 1993
ISBN 0 19 321866 6
Design and illustration by Creative Intelligence, Bristol
Printed in Great Britain by Caligraving Ltd., Thetford, Norfolk

Contents

There are nine books in this series:

Explore Music through

Art, Geography, History, Maths, Movement, Poetry and Rhyme, Science, Stories, Word Games.

Introduction

These booklets are designed for primary teachers who value the role of music in an integrated approach to the curriculum. They are of equal value to those who have little or no experience of teaching music, or those who have responsibility as a music co-ordinator.

By closely relating musical activities to other areas of the curriculum, it is hoped that primary teachers will feel more confident when engaging in musical activities with children.

Within each of the nine booklets in the series, activities are ordered progressively from 'early years' through to upper Key Stage 2.

The appropriateness of any activity will depend on the previous experience of the child or group. For this reason we have not recommended any activity for a specific age group, but have indicated a target Key Stage.

Many activities, especially those primarily concerned with composition, are often best delivered over a number of sessions. This allows time for exploratory work, and also for evaluation, discussion, and development.

Building a Repertoire of Sounds

Children need an ever-increasing knowledge of sounds, and teachers need to be aware of the importance of sound exploration for future musical activities. This repertoire of sounds is especially important when children wish to represent feelings, objects, and other sounds in their compositions.

Body and Vocal Sounds

Children should explore the possibility for sounds made both vocally and with the body. For instance, how many sounds can be made with the throat? ('Ooooh', 'Ahhhh', a hiccup, a cough, a gargle, humming, sighing, panting, etc.) What different sounds can be made by patting different parts of the body? (Cheeks, chest, stomach, thighs, knees, etc.)

Classroom Percussion

Children should be encouraged to find as many different ways as possible to play percussion. Can it be scraped, tapped, shaken, scratched, blown, etc.? When a new sound is found, think about what moods or images it conjures up. Such exploration works well in small groups, using a limited number of instruments. Allow the children time to play new sounds to the rest of the class.

Percussion Resources

Some considerations when building resources:

Do your percussion resources offer a wide choice for creating a variety of sounds?

Are the instruments made from a variety of materials (e.g. wood, metal, plastic, etc.)?

Does the collection contain instruments from different ethnic origins?

Are the instruments of good quality? Remember, as in other areas of the curriculum, poor quality materials (e.g. worn or broken) may lead to poor or disappointing results.

Other Sound Makers

A wide variety of sounds can be made with everyday objects such as paper, kitchen utensils, beads and pulses (e.g. paper tearing, scrunching, flapping; pulses poured into a bucket, swirled around, shaken; pots and pans drum-kit).

When performing any activity, try different combinations of sound, as this adds to the children's exploratory work, and their understanding of timbre and texture.

Recording

It is very important that children develop ways of recording their compositions. A variety of ways are suggested throughout the booklets, for example, pictures, symbols, words, letters, and so on. Ensure paper and appropriate recording materials are always available.

Audio as well as video recorders are also valuable resources for recording children's work and development.

The Activities

Suggested Materials

These materials should be useful as a guide for preparing the lessons. They are only suggestions and teachers may wish to select their own materials.

Attainment Target Boxes

The left-hand box gives an indication of the main focus of each activity, relating to the national curriculum for Music. However it should be noted that the activities will also offer a variety of other musical experiences.

The right-hand box indicates how the activity may complement work undertaken in another area of the curriculum.

Classroom Organization

For many whole-class activities, a circle of children on a carpet or chairs is ideal. This helps concentration and promotes a feeling of involvement, as well as being practical when it comes to observing other children, whole-group involvement, and passing games. It might be advisable at times to split the class or set into groups.

There are some activities that require little or no percussion, and if you are just starting out you may feel more confident attempting these activities initially.

Handing Out Instruments

Avoid the children making a headlong rush to the music trolley at all costs! Allow the children to collect, or hand out, a few instruments at a time.

– Have the required instruments placed out ready beforehand.
– While listening to instructions, children should place their instruments on the floor in front of them.
– Give out beaters for instruments last.
– Before commencing agree on clear signals for stopping and putting instruments down (e.g. a hand in the air, a finger to the lips, a wink of the eye, etc.).
– Demand an immediate response to these signals.
– Encourage children to treat instruments with respect at all times. (This is not easy if instruments are worn or broken.)

Evaluation and Appraisal

When children are working on a composition, there should be regular evaluation by the teacher, and/or by the children, of how the work is progressing. This will include a great deal of purposeful listening and appraising. The process will in turn help the children in appraising the music of others.

Key Questions for Performers and Audience

Can you tell us about your music?

How did the piece start/finish?

What did you like about it?

What contrasts/changes did the piece contain?

Does the piece fulfil the task set?

Was it performed fluently and appropriately?

Could it have been improved, and if so, how?

Could the piece be extended, and if so, how? (e.g. repetition, contrasts, new material, different instruments, etc.)

Did the audience listen well?

What Comes Next?

Suggested Materials

Four or five different instruments.

This activity is very similar to the game 'I went to Market and I bought . . .' except that instead of building a list, the children build a sequence of sounds. Choose one child to go first. (Children sit in a circle, with the instruments in the middle.)

1. The first child goes to the middle, picks up an instrument, makes a short sound, replaces the instrument, and returns to his/her place.

2. The next child in the circle repeats the first sound and adds a second one. Child 3 plays sound 1, sound 2 then adds a third sound, and so on. The same instrument(s) may be played more than once within any sequence. (At the early stage remembering the sequence of instruments is more important than imitating the exact sound, which can be quite hard.) It is best not to spend more than a few minutes on this activity, but to repeat it regularly. If you have a large class divide it into groups.

Music Attainment Target: 1 & 2
Main Focus: Sound Sequencing
Key Stage: 1

Maths Attainment Target: 3
Main Focus: Pattern

How Loud?

Suggested Materials

Pictures of animals or teacher's/children's drawings. A selection of instruments and other sound makers.

1. Play two contrasting instruments. Agree with the children which is the louder, which the quieter. (Obviously this will depend on how the instrument is played.) Repeat with other instruments and place them into two sets.

2. Show the children the musical symbols for loud (f) and quiet (p). The two sets could be marked with the musical symbols for loud and soft.

3. Introduce a category for instruments that are neither loud nor quiet. (The musical symbol for this category can be mf – moderately loud.)

4. Record results on a block graph (see activity '**Sets and Symbols**').

Extension Activities

Compose a short piece combining loud and quiet sounds. Record by using images such as a lion for loud and a butterfly for quiet. Ask the children what image they might use for moderately loud (e.g. sheep?).

Music Attainment Target: 1 & 2
Main Focus: Listening
Key Stage: 1

Maths Attainment Target: 5
Main Focus: Sorting

How Long?

Suggested Materials

Sheets of paper and something to draw with. Chime bars, cymbal, wood block, claves, Indian bells, triangle, tulip block, metallophone.

1. Choose an instrument with a long sound, e.g. a cymbal. Children put their hands in the air, and the teacher plays one beat on the cymbal. Allow the cymbal to resonate. Children put their hands down when they can no longer hear the sound of the cymbal resonating.

2. Now repeat with a short-sounding instrument, e.g. claves.

3. Continue with an assortment, classifying each one. Place instruments into two sorting hoops.

4. Repeat the sorting task, this time asking children to predict which group they think the instrument will belong to, before playing the instrument.

5. Can you produce short sounds on the instruments that formerly made long sounds? (e.g. touch the bar of the chime bar as you tap it).

Extension Activities

Compose brief pieces with long and short sounds. Record by drawing snakes for long sounds and tadpoles for short.

| Music Attainment Target: 1 & 2 |
| Main Focus: Listening |
| Key Stage: 1 |

| Maths Attainment Target: 5 |
| Main Focus: Sorting |

Tom's Morning

Suggested Materials

Percussion and other sound makers, body and vocal sounds.

1. Talk to the children about their morning routine before each day at school. What do they do? In what order?

2. Introduce Tom (a fictional character) and describe his routine showing the appropriate times on a teaching clock.

    8.00 a.m. – Gets up

    8.15 a.m. – Breakfast

    8.30 a.m. – Journey to school

    9.00 a.m. – School starts

3. Think of sounds to illustrate each stage, e.g.

    Getting up – water running (glockenspiel), brushing teeth (cabasa, maracas), brushing hair (brushed cymbal)

    Breakfast – kettle (hissing vocal sounds), snap crackle pop, cutlery and pottery sounds (pots and pans, etc. tapped and rattled . . .)

    Journey – footsteps, chattering, birds singing, car horns

    School – bell rings

4. Using a teaching clock, slowly move the hands around from 8.00 to 9.00. The children play the appropriate sounds at the appropriate time.

Extension Activities

Perhaps the whole piece could start with an alarm clock, and with footsteps continuing throughout the piece.

Music Attainment Target: 1 Main Focus: Composing Key Stage: 1	Maths Attainment Target: 2 Main Focus: Time

Dotty

Suggested Materials

Cards (see below). Selection of instruments.

1. Display a selection of the 'Dotty' cards (see below).
2. Point to the cards one after the other. The children clap once for each dot on the card you are pointing to.
3. Repeat the activity using other sounds (e.g. patting knees, short vocal sounds). The children could take turns to conduct by pointing at the cards.
4. Now repeat using instruments.

Extension Activities

Extend this activity to include ways of indicating whether the children should play loudly or quietly, e.g. use different coloured dots or mark cards with the symbols f (loud) and p (quiet).

Music Attainment Target: 1
Main Focus: Playing from Symbols
Key Stage: 1

Maths Attainment Target: 2
Main Focus: Number

Patterns

Suggested Materials

Pictures of instruments that the children can arrange (see below), plus the corresponding instruments.

1. The children select cards for two instruments. They arrange these cards into a short repeating pattern. The children play from left to right, playing when it is their turn, e.g.

2. As the children gain an understanding of this they can go on to make more elaborate patterns with added instruments, which they can perform to the rest of the class, e.g.

3. Can the children listening to the sequences identify the repeated pattern?

Music Attainment Target: 1	Maths Attainment Target: 3
Main Focus: Composing and Recording Sequences	Main Focus: Pattern
Key Stage: 1	

Wait Your Turn

Suggested Materials

Scores (see below). Three or four types of instrument.

1. Hand out three types of instrument to the class (e.g. drums, claves, tambourines). If you do not have one for each child, work with a group. The children with instruments follow the score, making a sound on their instrument for each dot.

2. In the second score groups of notes are separated by vertical lines. This is a device in music called 'bars' which makes following the score easier. To help counting and to feel the rhythm, the first beat is usually stronger (louder).

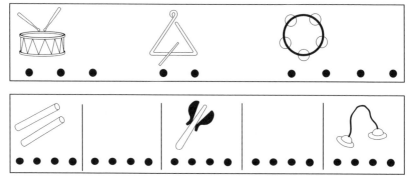

3. With the children, make up scores using different groupings, e.g. two, three, five, six, seven, etc.

Extension Activities

Some children might like to work in groups and produce their own scores to perform to the rest of the class.

Music Attainment Target: 1 Main Focus: Performing from Symbols Key Stage: 1/2	Maths Attainment Target: 2 Main Focus: Number

Geo-Scores

Suggested Materials

Selection of instruments.

Large sheets of paper and something to draw with.

1. Children use a shape to represent a sound, e.g.

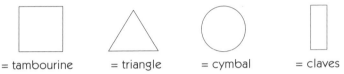

= tambourine   = triangle   = cymbal   = claves

2. Draw a score for the children to play from, e.g.

Don't worry if the children play more than one sound for their turn.

3. Children may like to draw their own scores, and perform them with friends to the rest of the class.

Extension Activities

Add other geometrical shapes, e.g. pentagon, hexagon.

Music Attainment Target: 1 Main Focus: Composing and Recording Key Stage: 1/2

Maths Attainment Target: 4 Main Focus: Shape

Soundchart

Suggested Materials

A selection of instruments and other sound makers.

Use comparative length and comparative volume to categorize instruments, as below.

LONG	LONGER	LONGEST
Triangle	Indian bells	Cymbal
Chime bar	Triangle	Bass drum

LOUD	LOUDER	LOUDEST
Indian bells	Claves	Bass drum
Tambourine	Tulip block	Cymbal

(Obviously judgements will depend on how each instrument is played. Some children might notice that an instrument's sound depends on the way it is played, and this can promote further useful discussion.)

Music Attainment Target: 2
Main Focus: Composing and Recording
Key Stage: 1/2

Maths Attainment Target: 5
Main Focus: Classifying

Sets and Symbols

Suggested Materials

A variety of percussion instruments. Sheets of paper, and something to draw with.

1. Begin with the sorting activity from '**How Long?**'. As more instruments are introduced the children may notice that a third category starts to appear. These could be placed in a third group of instruments that are not long or short in resonance.

2. Once sorted, the children could make a block graph of their findings.

Long	Medium	Short

(Are there any other ways of recording?)

3. Can the children find a way of expressing 'long', 'medium' and 'short', with a symbol for each one? For example:

long =

medium =

short =   •

4. Ask the children to invent a sequence using their symbols and appropriate instruments. Remember to repeat some of the sounds, e.g.

Start   Finish

Extension Activities

Once the children have completed this activity, they could then consider the volume, e.g. if dots increase in size this indicates an increase in volume.

Music Attainment Target: 2	Maths Attainment Target: 5
Main Focus: Appraising and Recording	Main Focus: Recording Data
Key Stage: 1/2	

Spreadsheet

Suggested Materials

A selection of instruments and other sound makers.

Classify the sounds using the criteria below in the Carroll diagram.
(Obviously this will depend on how the instruments are played, and is
relative to the selection of instruments available.)

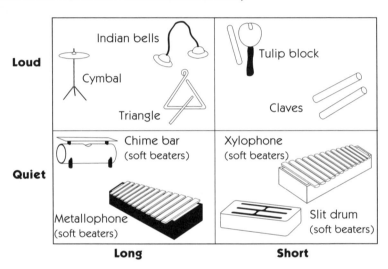

Extension Activities

Compose short pieces combining different lengths and volumes. Use
symbols from previous activities, e.g.

Music Attainment Target: 2	Maths Attainment Target: 5
Main Focus: Appraising	Main Focus: Recording Data
Key Stage: 1/2	

And So On . . .

Suggested Materials

Tuned percussion, e.g. xylophone, glockenspiel.

1. As for activity '**What Comes Next?**', but this time the children build up a sequence of notes, e.g.

High

High, low

High, low, low . . . and so on.

This activity should start very simply, using just two of the bars, e.g. the lowest and highest. (It may help to remove the redundant bars, but do not move remaining bars from their correct position – see below.)

2. As the children improve, build up the number of notes (e.g. three bars and/or closer pitch range).

(Once this activity is established it can work well in small groups.)

Music Attainment Target: 1 & 2	Maths Attainment Target: 3
Main Focus: Composing Sequences	Main Focus: Pattern
Key Stage: 1/2	

Pitch Points

Suggested Materials

Tuned percussion. Notation cards (see below).

1. Show the children the following four cards.

2. Choose a high note to represent the high dot, and a low note to represent the low dot. Play each card in turn, so that the children can match the sound to the symbols.

3. Now play one of the cards. Can the children identify which card was played?

4. Once this activity has been established, a middle pitch can be introduced, e.g.

Extension Activities

The children may write their own cards and arrange them to make a short melody to perform to the rest of the class.

Music Attainment Target: 1 & 2
Main Focus: Recording Pitch
Key Stage: 2

Maths Attainment Target: 3
Main Focus: Pattern

Down on the Farm

Suggested Materials
Selection of instruments.

(Children in a circle.)

1. The children choose a number between one and four. Then they choose a sound (farmyard noises are good fun). The chosen sound should be a single sound, e.g. 'quack' as opposed to 'cock-a-doodle-doo'.

2. The teacher then counts '1 2 3 4' over and over, while the children make their sound on their chosen number. (It helps when starting off to 'count in', in other words a count of four before the children join in.)

3. Once this is going well, stop counting aloud. Can the children still keep the sequence together, and steady?

4. To create a moment of silence, repeat the activity asking the children not to choose number 3.

5. Try using different number patterns, e.g. counting from 1 to 5, 1 to 7, etc. With longer sequences of numbers, e.g. 1 to 9, children might like making their sound on two numbers, e.g. 2 and 7.

Extension Activities
Try the activities clapping, and then using instruments.

| Music Attainment Target: 1 |
| Main Focus: Pulse and Rhythm |
| Key Stage: 2 |

| Maths Attainment Target: 3 |
| Main Focus: Pattern |

Coconut Shy

Suggested Materials

Grid (see right), with stick-on picture cards.

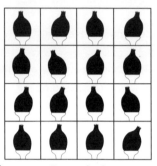

Example 1

1. The idea is for the children to clap if the squares have coconuts (all squares at first). The score should be followed to a steady pulse, reading a row at a time from left to right. Initially help the children by pointing, but then encourage them to keep an internal pulse. (Example 1)

2. Once this can be done successfully, coconuts can be 'knocked off', leaving a silent space. (Example 2)

3. Repeat the above activity using coconuts of two different colours each assigned to a different group. One group of children clap on their colour, the other group on theirs.

4. Now try different grids, e.g. 5 x 5, 7 x 7, 9 x 9.

Example 2

Extension Activities

Children could be given blank grids to invent their own pieces, using instruments of their choice, which they can perform to the rest of the group. Try with two groups performing simultaneously.

Music Attainment Target: 1
Main Focus: Playing to the Pulse
Key Stage: 2

Maths Attainment Target: 2
Main Focus: Number

Hiking

(For this activity you will need a large space, e.g. the hall or playground. Children initially in a circle.)

1. The children number off from 1 to 4 round the circle, going clockwise or anti-clockwise. The children say their number while maintaining a steady pulse (regular beat). (N.B. This requires frequent practice.)
2. Now try again with number '1' saying his/her number loudly, while the others say theirs quietly.
3. Now the children walk freely around the hall, stamping on the strong beat, e.g.

   1 2 3 4 *1* 2 3 4 *1* 2 3 4 *1* 2 3 4

4. Repeat the activity at a different speed. Is it harder to maintain a slow pace or a fast pace?

Extension Activities

Transfer to instruments. The children play when they say their number, number 1 still playing louder. Now try without counting aloud.

Try other number sequences (e.g. 1–6, 1–8).

Also try sequences such as: 1–3, 1– 5, 1–7.

Do the children notice when walking to this pattern that number 1 comes on alternate feet?

Music Attainment Target: 1
Main Focus: Pulse
Key Stage: 2

Maths Attainment Target: 2
Main Focus: Number

Tap Tap Clap Clap

(Children in a circle.)

1. The children set up a sequence e.g. tap knees x 2, clap hands x 2. This should be done to a steady pulse of '1 2 3 4'. (Remember to count in.)

2. Now, instead of clapping twice leave a space, i.e. 'tap, tap, — , — ' (The children might find it helpful to tap the air on these silent beats.)

3. In the gap each child says his/her name in turn (e.g. tap tap Pe-ter). Try to say the names rhythmically. (Discuss with the children why some names are more difficult to fit in than others – such as 'Ra-ha-na'.)

4. Next, try the same activity, but this time the children fill the gaps with names of pop groups, favourite foods, etc.

Extension Activities

The above activity can be tried with different sequences, such as

'tap, tap, tap, ?, ?'

'tap, ?, ?'

'tap, tap, tap, tap, ?, ?'

This activity could also be repeated using multiplication bonds, e.g. 'tap, tap, 3, –; tap, tap, 6, –; tap , tap, 9, –; tap, tap, 12, –; tap, tap, fif-teen,' and so on (all children tapping and saying the numbers together).

Music Attainment Target: 1 Main Focus: Pulse and Rhythm Key Stage: 2	Maths Attainment Target: 2 Main Focus: Number

Bonds

Suggested Materials
Number charts.
A variety of instruments.

1. This is similar to the maths activity where children colour in numbers on a grid in, say, the x 2 table and the x 3 table. Here the children clap or play on their number. In chart A the numbers to play are those in a circle (x 2).

2. Try the same activity with x 3 and x 4.

3. Try combinations (charts B & C), with children in groups. The children all start together, but some will only clap on a circle, others on a square, and so on.

Discuss the results, e.g. what do the children notice about the numbers where everyone plays? Are any numbers silent? Are they prime numbers?

A

1	2	3	4	5	6
7	8	9	10	11	12
13	14	15	16	17	18
19	20	21	22	23	24

B

1	2	3	4	5	6
7	8	9	10	11	12
13	14	15	16	17	18
19	20	21	22	23	24

C

1	2	3	4	5	6
7	8	9	10	11	12
13	14	15	16	17	18
19	20	21	22	23	24

Extension Activities
Repeat the activity using instruments. Can the children produce their own pieces using other multiplication bonds?

Music Attainment Target: 1
Main Focus: Pulse and Rhythm
Key Stage: 2

Maths Attainment Target: 2
Main Focus: Number

Ready Steady Go

Suggested Materials

Number chart (see below).

1. Follow the top line only. The children clap on every number in a circle (odd numbers) while the teacher leads by pointing to each number in turn, or counts from 1 to 8, at a steady pulse. Repeat until the children have the rhythm. (Remember to count in.)

(1)	2	(3)	4	(5)	6	(7)	8
1	(2)	3	(4)	5	(6)	7	(8)
(1)	(2)	3	4	(5)	(6)	7	8
1	2	(3)	(4)	5	6	(7)	(8)
(1)	2	3	(4)	(5)	6	(7)	8

2. Now do the same for line two (even numbers).

3. Split the class in two, one group clapping the top line over and over, the other following line two. The teacher should assist at first by counting out loud, but gradually fade, leaving the children to keep their own internal pulse.

4. Try adding other lines, such as lines three and four above (harder), and line five (much harder).

5. Try the activity at a faster or slower pace.

Extension Activities

Try the same activity with percussion. This is harder than clapping and will need practice. Some instruments are harder than others. Why is this?

Some children may like to create their own scores.

Music Attainment Target: 1 Main Focus: Pulse and Rhythm Key Stage: 2

Maths Attainment Target: 2 Main Focus: Number

Square Numbers

Suggested Materials

Number charts (see below). Selection of instruments.

1. The children clap the circled dots of one of the squares while the teacher leads by pointing to each dot in turn. (Remember that uncircled dots are silent beats.) Now practise some of the other square numbers in the same way.

2. Split the set so that one group claps one square and the second group another. Choose a child to lead the second group. Counting in is quite difficult. Try 'Off we go and . . .' (instead of '1 2 3 4'). It may well help to have a pulse keeper, e.g. a drum, a metronome, or the pulse from an electronic keyboard. What do the children notice? (e.g. When do claps coincide?)

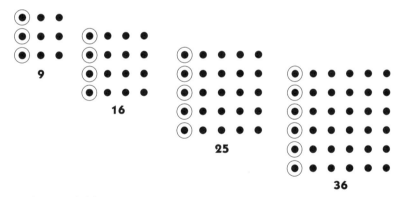

Extension Activities

Try the same activity with percussion instruments.

Music Attainment Target: 1	Maths Attainment Target: 2
Main Focus: Pulse and Rhythm	Main Focus: Square Numbers
Key Stage: 2	

Melody Chains

Suggested Materials

Tuned percussion, e.g. xylophones, metallophones, glockenspiels.

1. Ask the children to make up some short tunes, e.g.

   Tune 1: A - G - E - G -

   Tune 2: E - D - E - C - etc.

   Two tunes could be played alternately, e.g.

   A - G - E - G - /E - D - E - C - /A - G - E - G . . . and so on.

2. Try making a pattern of the two tunes, e.g.

   Tune 1, Tune 2, Tune 1,

   or try adding a third tune, e.g.

   Tune 1, Tune 2, Tune 1, Tune 3, Tune 1, Tune 2, Tune 1

Music Attainment Target: 1 & 2 Main Focus: Melody and Form Key Stage: 2	Maths Attainment Target: 3 Main Focus: Pattern

Musical Symmetry

Suggested Materials

Tuned percussion. Large sheets of paper and something to draw with.

1. Experiment, and find out what happens when a pattern is written out and then reflected. In the example below a six-note tune is shown in the first box in its original state, then reflected and/or rotated in the other three boxes.

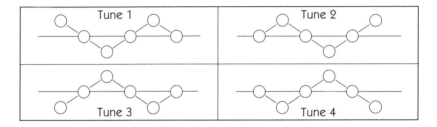

2. As in '**Melody Chains**' these resulting sequences may be ordered and used to produce a short piece, e.g.

Tune 1, Tune 2, Tune 1, Tune 3, Tune 1, Tune 4, Tune 1.

Music Attainment Target: 1 & 2
Main Focus: Melody and Form
Key Stage: 2

Maths Attainment Target: 4
Main Focus: Symmetry

Appendix

Glossary

Crescendo	Getting louder.
Decrescendo	Getting quieter.
Drone	One or more notes maintained throughout a piece.
Dynamics	The gradations of volume in music.
Form	The order in which different ideas appear in a piece of music.
Improvisation	Composing spontaneously while performing.
Glissando	The process of moving from one note to another quickly, while playing all other notes in between.
Notation	The symbolic written representation of sound(s).
Ostinato	A rhythm or melody pattern repeated regularly during a piece of music (often as accompaniment).
Pitch	The perception of sounds as 'high' or 'low' in relation to each other. A woman's voice is usually higher in pitch than a man's.
Pulse	A repetitive, regular beat (sometimes silent), which can indicate the speed of a piece of music.
Rest	'Musical silence' – the absence of a sounding note or notes.
Rhythm	The pattern which long and short sounds and rests make when heard in sequence.
Rhythmic independence	The ability to maintain a rhythm against other rhythms.
Score	A written record of all the parts in a piece of music.
Sequencing	The ordering of sounds.
Timbre	The characteristics/colour of sound(s).
Volume	

Symbols

f	Loud
p	Quiet
<	Getting louder
>	Getting quieter

Pentatonic Scales

The notes on tuned percussion should be arranged with long bars to the left, getting increasingly smaller to the right-hand side, and in alphabetical order. Most (but not all) start with 'C'.

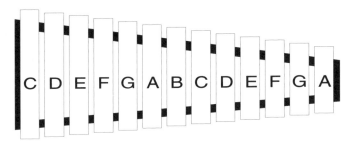

By removing any note 'B' and any note 'F', it is possible to have a five-note scale, called 'Pentatonic' (Penta = five). This should leave a sequence of C D E G A.

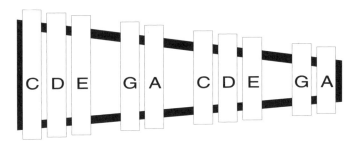

A pentatonic scale is useful for improvising melodies, both solo and in group work.

Occasionally instruments will come with notes called 'sharps' (with a ♯ after the letter), and 'flats' (with a ♭ after the letter), e.g. C♯ E♭ F♯ G♯ B♭. By using only these notes, it is again possible to create a pentatonic scale. This same scale can be found by just using the black notes on a piano or keyboard. Use this scale if most of the notes on your tuned percussion are sharps and flats.

Teacher's Notes